D0341322

WITHDRAWN

Riffs & Reciprocities

ALSO BY STEPHEN DUNN

poetry:

Loosestrife
New & Selected Poems, 1974–1994
Landscape at the End of the Century
Between Angels
Local Time
Not Dancing
Work & Love
A Circus of Needs
Full of Lust and Good Usage
Looking for Holes in the Ceiling

prose:

Walking Light: Essays & Memoirs

. . . .

Stephen Dunn

W. W. NORTON & COMPANY

NEW YORK / LONDON

Riffs
&
Reciprocities

PROSE PAIRS

T 124835

VISTA GRANDE
PUBLIC LIBRARY

Copyright © 1998 by Stephen Dunn

All rights reserved
Printed in the United States of America
First Edition

For information about permission to reproduce selections from this book, write
to Permissions, W. W. Norton & Company, Inc., 500 Fifth Avenue, New York,
NY 10110.

The text of this book is composed in Janson
with the display set in Caslon 540
Composition and manufacturing by the Haddon Craftsmen, Inc.
Book design by JAM Design

Library of Congress Cataloging-in-Publication Data

Dunn, Stephen, 1939–
Riffs and reciprocities : prose pairs / by Stephen Dunn.
p.   cm.
ISBN 0-393-04630-3
I. Title.
PS3554.U49R54   1998
814'.54—dc21   97-31238
CIP

W. W. Norton & Company, Inc., 500 Fifth Avenue, New York, N.Y. 10110
http://www.wwnorton.com

W. W. Norton & Company Ltd., 10 Coptic Street, London WC1A 1PU

1 2 3 4 5 6 7 8 9 0

For Claire Gerber

Contents

III

Acknowledgments

The American Poetry Review: Bourgeois/Religion, Reflection/Shadow, Insurance/Luck, Irony/Earnestness, Syntax/Mimesis

Fugue: Fog/Luminescence, Outlaw/Citizen

The Georgia Review: Technology/Memory, Emblems/Heroes, Anger/Generosity, Experts/Ignorance, Intoxication/Habit, Scruples/Saints, Obstinacy/Principles, Passion/Paradox, Faces/Bodies, Sky/Weather

Green Mountains Review: Information/Personal

Harper's Magazine: reprinted "Scruples" from *The Georgia Review*

Kenyon Review: Democracy/Rights, Hegemony/Honor, Frivolity/Seriousness, Legacy/Silence

Mid-American Review: Midnight/Noon

Poetry Northwest: "Seriousness" in a different form

Shenandoah: Evil/Advocacy, Mercy/Vengeance

The Southern Review: Defeats/Acceptance, Anonymity/Indifference, Vulgar/Sublime, Strangers/Acquaintances, Money/Indulgence, Suicides/Funerals, Cynicism/Ego, Ambition/Humility,

Reading/Erasure, Superstition/Certainty,
Landscapes/Interiors, Hypocrisy/Precision,
Despair/Illness, Natives/Lovers, Scapegoat/Criminal

Talking River Review: Bedroom/Kitchen,
Advantages/Superiority

My thanks to The Rockefeller Foundation (Bellagio) and to Yaddo where many of these pairs were composed. And to Richard Stockton College for a summer grant. And, once again, to my loyal and careful readers: Sam Toperoff, Lawrence Raab, Carol Houck Smith, Philip Booth, Gregory Djanikian, Joe-Anne McLaughlin-Carruth, and my wife, Lois. A special thanks to Claire Gerber, to whom this book is dedicated, who gave me the idea for writing about things and ideas that might be tangentially related.

Preface

After my friend Claire asked me if I would do some thinking for her about the differences between "Reflection" and "Shadow," and I did, I became intrigued with working in tangentially related pairs, each a discrete paragraph and as packed and pithy as I could fashion. Sometimes an act of definition or redefinition, sometimes a description or occasional story, sometimes both, I began to see them as extensions of the the poetry I'd been writing off and on for many years—in which I tried to pin down an abstraction or breathe a personal life into it. I'd read the prose poems of Ponge and Michaux, Pascal's *Pensées*, the elegant and compelling miniatures of Calvino. I was attracted by such vehicles for meditation and exploration, and the compositional pressures they exerted to make every sentence count. But no one, to my knowledge, had worked in pairs, and the more I worked that way the more I became fascinated with how I might make different ideas, claims, and stories rub up against and inform each other. The notion of writing a riff on something, while liberating in certain ways, forced a commitment to rhythm and flow that was pleasingly demanding. And each riff "found" its reciprocity; I rarely began a paragraph knowing what the next paragraph would be. In a dream the other night, I told Claire that the mind is the body's tagalong, that the body is always planning a fiesta. "Of course," she said, "that's why civilizations try to subjugate the body." Then she said, "Enough of abstractions, I'm hungry for Buicks and re-frigerators, Jack cheese and sycamores, words like that." To use them in sentences quieted her. She just listened. The next day I called, and told Claire the dream. "Working on those prose pairs again?" she said, without the question mark.

Poems should be more like essays and essays should
be more like poems.
—CHARLES OLSON

Two of every sort shall thou bring into the Ark.
—GENESIS

I

. . .

Technology

. . .

Maybe we've always been transported by what we can't explain. But if the world were almost destroyed and only a few of us remained, who could reinvent the telephone, no less the radio or the car? I'd be a man with hopes for a farm. I turn the television on, and there's Baghdad, and there's a missile and a rationale. I could be in a cave watching the Northern Lights—it's all so out of my control. I watch a laser repair a heart. I look in at my daughter before she's born. There used to be a gulf between empiricism and faith. Now an e-mail message arrives on my turned-off machine. Somebody who lives in cyberspace—where my mother never roamed—could say how. Normal: the most malleable word our century has known. The light bulb changed the evening. The car invented the motel.

Memory

A kind of achievement, William Carlos Williams said. Or a curse, said the man who couldn't get the phone book out of his head. Speak, Nabokov asked of his. Which it tends to, if we invoke it often enough. Imagination is its most important friend, selecting, coloring, casting aside. Without imagination, an endlessness, like my colleague's story of his summer by the lake when he listed birds and his wife was tortured by a lingering cold; he told me so much I didn't know what I'd been told. More and more I forget what I need, and remember what I'd like to forget. And sometimes I keep talking, keep recalling, as a way of not saying what I feel. Memory's law: what we choose to say about our past becomes our past. That other past, the one we've lived, exists in pieces that flicker and grow dim. I can buy memory in a store called Circuit City. I can press search, and find a fact, a person, but not what I've most dearly lost. Every time I save I exclude.

. . .

Scruples

. . .

Since the early eighties more students in my Literature &
Ethics class, a freshman seminar, say they would press a button that would kill a nondescript peasant in another land,
for which they would receive one million dollars and the
guarantee of never being caught. They respond anony-
mously and must give a reason. Four out of twenty-five
would in 1982. Eleven out of twenty-five in 1995. Reasons:
Because it would set me up for life. Or, It's just a one-time
thing. And once, Because it's a doggie-dog world. Afterward,
I point out that the question is designed only to see if they
are murderers. By semester's end, I'm pretty sure I know
who they are, these murderers, and it all switches to me—
that age-old imperative, to discover what's right and to do it.
I've given a murderer an A because of incontrovertible intelligence. Yet I've graded down at least a few because their
logic, however sound, was without heart and I didn't like
their faces. And I can't say how many times I've given up on
some of the decent ones—their correct, inherited, annoying
positions unchanged by drama or dialectic. In the early sev-
enties, no one I knew would press the button. I love that it
wasn't high-mindedness back then, merely the obvious, and
that so many wished to do good. Experience took years to
show us what we could not sustain.

Saints

Those who earn their names know what suffering is . . . and elect it anyway. They love without ambivalence one shining thing, yet some—the even more saintly—are tortured by the manifold richness of the discernible world. I've known one secular saint. I watched him fast so an idea would swell. I didn't want to be him, though once or twice, by design, I've felt that strange sumptuousness born from doing without. For him it must have been an imagined feast, like a wafer on the tongue. For me: just another something for the body to have known before it dies and becomes dust. Saints, like revolutionaries, walk headlong into the cool, dry wind, are always serving a hidden flame, are terrifying because of what they do not need. The saint asks, What will you die for? The revolutionary adds, For what would you kill? Either way, sacrifice is an ugly business, as ugly as history itself. Choose between these terrible things, history often says. We are only commentators until, for us, it comes to that choice.

. . .

Evil

. . .

The best teacher I had in college criticized my use of "inhuman." In the margin, he wrote, "When it comes to that, human will do just fine." Later, I had no trouble believing that Pol Pot's crimes "against humanity" were human, as were, say, Jeffrey Dahmer's murders and dismemberments. Like Hitler, Pol Pot thought he had good reasons, which most of us do. Dahmer was just nuts, which is human as well. A Khmer Rouge torturer said, "Once we have beaten the enemies for a long time, they are in pain even when they aren't being beaten. They're in pain and so skinny that it's no longer possible to beat them. Thus we get only a little information." Then, after a pause, "One person had confessed a good deal, but when he swallowed nails we had to spend good time and good medicine to treat him. The Party is poor, and these expenses are difficult to meet." My teacher called himself a humanist. Dark, brooding man, he loved those big Russian novels in which no one is left unscarred, and the heartless and the decent suffer about equally.

Advocacy

Always a little more fun on the Devil's side. I've been his advocate, have opposed what I most believed, testing if what I believed was true. It sometimes almost was; that's the best I can say. But you can bedevil yourself if you keep playing that game. You don't want to stand in a torturer's shoes for long. Still, when it comes to seeking a truth, a certain cruelty can go a long way—right through the heart of a thing to some other side. Doesn't every far-reaching truth cause a lesser truth to die? Most of us are content to stop at the heart. When I've been good's advocate, playing the less clever role, I've gone as far as good can go. Maybe some orthodoxy or some abomination lost ground for a while. Maybe not. The one time I had the Devil down, thinking he'd give, he whispered, "Remember, the punishment for being good is a life of goodness." I laughed, and he was gone.

. . .

Intoxication

. . .

That sensation of "fine excess" Keats wanted from poetry, the adjective gracing the noun, keeping it alert. I like intoxicated *with* more than intoxicated *by*. Either with drink or with thou, I always want a person at the end, nearby. *Both*, though, is my kind of intoxicant's choice. There are ways of changing what capacity means. Long training, for one, like an athlete finding his best time. Oh to have a best time again and again. Sloppiness ruins it all, the person and the time. Both. Interesting, how context surrounds and informs, how it can make a good word bad. To create one's own context: that's always taken two gods, the wild one and the orderly conjurer of shapes. I drink to each. At worst, the intoxicant becomes the drunk, magnifies something awful in himself, manufactures an excuse. I hope I'll never need to drown one more thing or—that other sorrow—to turn toward sobriety.

Habit

Without it, Aristotle said, there can be no virtue. He meant no single act could make us virtuous, that virtue had to be proven over time. I suppose he wouldn't even think it funny if I, trying to claim a place for myself in the murky realm of ethics, said that for years I've had two drinks before dinner— an act of moderation by my standards—and have done little harm to self and world. No doubt he'd be happier if someone had said let's steal a car and I'd said no immediately, which I would have done—also out of long habit, good habits being what he had in mind. Of course, all I'd need is a sufficient context—my injured wife in need of transportation, say—and virtue would once again be fun. Another ethicist then might have it hinge on what I did with the car afterward, perhaps on what reparation I'd make. Philosophical jazz. The mind at serious play. Habit—in the Aristotelian sense—can free us from thought. Usually I don't think, one way or another, about two drinks before dinner. I would have to think about a third, which raises the issue of bad habits and when they begin. I know more than two things about bad habits, but here are two. Shame, not reason, is their revisionist. We cling to them as Sophists clung to their last shreds of truth.

· · ·

Bourgeois

. . .

What we would never let ourselves become, tra la. Especially a petit. Wasn't the edge the only place to be? Or of the working class, which would rise someday. Startling that it rose, without rancor, happily in fact, toward the bourgeoisie. Startling, too: capitalism's elasticity, that fat boy with quick feet, subtly accommodating, and not quite there when we swung. In a few long years we'd be his wary friend. We'd own mutual funds. Our property was our property, and fences were good. Parents now, we offered "Be carefuls" as often as we once cried, "Fascist pigs." Oh not petit, but grand! So what if we believed in the efficacies of art, and still spoke about souls? So what if we still resisted the God-fearing and the Republicans and a few of their little, dispiriting rules? Each year we felt less and less dislocated at the mall. We used our remotes without irony and for entire evenings hardly moved.

Religion

First, it was more about mystery than about trying to get us
to behave. Whichever, we're still in some lonely cave, not far
from that moment a lightning storm or a sunset drove us to
invent the upper reaches of the sky. Religion is proof that a
good story, well-told, is a powerful thing. Proof, too, that
terror makes fabulists of us all. We're pitiful, finally, and so
oddly valiant. The dead god rising into ism after ism—that
longing for coherence that keeps us, if not naive, historically
challenged. To love Christ you must love the Buddha, to love
Mohammed or Moses you must love Confucius and, say,
Schopenhauer and Nietzsche as well. They were all wise and
unsponsored and insufficient, some of the best of us. I'm saying this to myself: the sacred cannot be found unless you
give up some old version of it. And when you do, mon sem-
blable, mon frère, I swear there'll be an emptiness it'll take a
lifetime to fill. Indulge, become capacious, give up nothing,
Jack my corner grocer said. He was pushing the portobellos,
but I was listening with that other, my neediest ear.

. . .

Passion

. . .

The Last Supper over, Christ's long night about to begin: suffering was what passion meant. Just vestiges of that meaning now; our lovers' contorted mouths, their groans—what might be, if we didn't know better, pain. Strange though, conjoined, how solitary we can be, how up on some fabulous cross. "To be acted upon by an external force," the dictionary says, and we understand: a loveliness in league with awe removing us from control. Christ's suffering, though, had such a brilliant passivity, it changed the world. Mine often has been bloodless, small: after passion to live with the encroachment of the acceptable, the evenly keeled. But when passion has failed, I've felt myself watching from some tower in myself, half-bemused, in the act of an act, in remove. Come morning I've put on my suit and made my way—sensibly in check—toward my job. Most of us know this: it hasn't been difficult at all.

Paradox

"If you fear loneliness," Chekhov wrote, "then marriage is not for you," and I understood paradox could give a kind of relief, mixed feelings at last getting their due. More aggressive than ambiguity, paradox breaks in, disturbs our conventional sense of things. It's the jolt that gives us permission to think what in fact we've thought. When Dali said, "The difference between me and a madman is that I'm not mad," what artist who's ever fractured and reordered experience didn't feel he had a friend? Only passion can make us feel as momentarily freed as paradox can. But paradox also does less consoling work. When I read Nietzsche's claim: "All that's ripe wants to die," I instantly knew how green I was, how far away from a fullness that might quiet me. I loved it nonetheless. As a jazzman once said, it hurt me good.

. . .

Money

. . .

Like a religion but without a theology, or a place to rest. And
as many or more bad things done in its name. Many minis-
ters of spin in its higher realms. Many priests of more. At its
most efficient and neutral: a form of exchange, eliminating
the three cows for their equivalent in grain. At its best: a
conduit to food and shelter and that little extra which trans-
lates into choice. Never to be coveted, though, unless we
wish only things in return. No correlation between savings
and saved. But money *is* power, and a kind of truth. We must
therefore distrust the truth, we lovers of truth. Make our
own. Once we thought our pockets should be empty, which
made us poor and righteous, not distrustful enough of thinking that wished to unite labor and need. We didn't know
enough about biology, or comfort's lure. Yet we were so naive
our errors had a beauty to them and bought us a few price-
less years.

Indulgence

Because, as Blake says, you have to know what's more than enough in order to know what's enough, we have a rationale if we need one. Or if more is required, "The road of excess leads to the palace of wisdom" has to it a pleasing economy that persuades. Let's run away to Bimini, wipe the bank account clean. But if there is a palace of wisdom, on its door it's sure to have: *There are many ways.* Next to excess, there must be: *Pare down, become lean.* Who's to say that the monk isn't indulging himself with glorious severities? Oh we know the penalties for serious indulgence: unrelieved pleasure for the hedonist, clarity's pain for the ascetic. But for most of us, indulgence falls short of a calling. We neither get wise from it nor especially ruined. A night on the town, halfway up the road.

. . .

Democracy

. . .

Appalling that some people—the mendacious, the uninformed—can vote. Yet worse if they could not. Oddly, the majority does have an intelligence, sleepy-keen, animal-like, most brilliant when injured or wronged. Huey Long, for example, was loved by that animal until it knew to turn. After the votes were in, he said, "The people have spoken, the bastards." And there it was, one of democracy's successes—the loser walking away with a quip, no need for a coup. Every few years the bastards and the good guys get shuffled, redefined. Some, somehow, manage to survive the compromises and levelings of their jobs. We try to forget that they don't dare challenge the country's shibboleths, that even the powerful say "God willing" when they mean "if I can." We try to forget that capitalism itself makes more large decisions than any senator with a program or a dream. We go down to the firehouse near the creek on those Tuesdays in November. We sign in. One by one, we the imperfect have our say.

Rights

What if we had the right only to sound opinions? Ah, who's to judge? say the hoi polloi. The teacher in the classroom, perhaps. The expert in the machine shop. Some lifer with a record of fairness and the severity that arises out of long caring. If we didn't make sense, we'd lose our right to another opinion for, say, an hour. And never could we say, "Well, that's just my opinion," or "One opinion is as good as another" without losing a few days' rights. Could more generosity be expected in the face of the shameless? If we'd said something very stupid, well then we would have to do some work in the community, say with the mentally impaired. After all, having a sound opinion is merely a minor achievement, just the beginning of good thinking. It's the least we should expect of ourselves.

. . .

Obstinacy

. . .

On a cliff, say, of ideas. The erosion already begun, and for
us the sweet perversity of holding on. For no better reason
than what's falling is and has been ours. And we remember
how long our friends stayed with Marxism, their passionate
certitude. Don't we owe our passions an obstinacy or two?
Don't we need to dig in one last time? The truth is, of course,
we've often been insufferable. And, in so many instances,
wrong. Otherwise there'd be different names for us: People
of Conviction. Or the Principled. The best of us yield in
time. We do not stay the course after the loosened boulders
reach the chasm's floor. Some of us apologize to those we insisted were fools. Yes, from the outset we heard their argu-
ments. We recognized the unravelings of our own. But
history holds dear the fabulously obstinate, those Luthers
and Galileos and Magellans. Perhaps we were thinking, hoping, desperately hoping, that we too were onto something
time would make self-evident, that we too might be remembered for our courage and our will.

Principles

I admit to having none. I had them once, the usual shalls and shall nots. But I'd get variously obese with life, and they couldn't hold me in. Nor could I do honor to them, they were so easily disappointed. I believed of course that one should always keep a promise. But I learned—so I could still feel decent, I suppose—to take the *always* out. It is always good to take the *always* out. It's not that I want principles to disappear. I think I'd like them written in sand, perhaps in the morning, so they can be seen by the children on their way for a swim. For me, I'd like to keep around the ghost of them. So I'd remember what I was violating when the body and its heart once again insisted on their contrary ways. So I could apologize to those who held them partially, yet held them dear: friends, lovers, the only people we could deeply betray.

. . .

Vulgar

· · ·

Not always bad taste, but the exercise of taste without knowing the level above it. Ostentation, sometimes as small as a
wink. The gum chewer, of course, and the man with a wad of
bills. But the patronizer, too, the person who puts his hand
on your shoulder without respect, who honeys and buds and
dolls. Those who think sarcasm is wit. Gossipers who chirp
rather than confide with the proper malice and delight. Gold
chains. In fact any jewelry that suggests a personality disor-
der. Sometimes, though, the vulgar is not vulgar. Fuck, pussy,
cock, for example, when used lovingly. The beer with the
ballgame. The rude, wounded, shout in the corporate calm.

Sublime

Las Vegas. Shut in for a weekend with slots, roulette, black jack, craps. A little of one, a lot of the other. Women with outfits cut for whatever you might be thinking, though you're not much thinking of them. Keno during mealtime. Big tip for the Keno girl when you win. Dealers with blank faces. Ladies with blue hair, and their polyester men. A couple of thousand to lose. Family politics says okay. Says once a year all right to flirt with just enough destruction to make the armpits sweat, the mind delude itself that it's bold. Almost no sleep. A hundred on black on a whim. Another scotch. Bells going off, people being ruined. Two days. I love vulgarity for two days. On the morning of the third, a craving for something else. At the Grand Canyon I feel nothing, and it feels fine. Silence. Beauty. A solid boredom taking hold.

· · ·

Syntax

. . .

"South played low from dummy on the first spade, and East took the king and returned a spade. South then led a diamond to finesse with the queen, but West gathered in the king and cashed three more spades. Down one. 'What could I do but try the diamond finesse?' South asked. North was too polite to answer." Clearly, Sheinwold, the Bridge expert, had a shapely mind. Because I didn't understand Bridge, my pleasures were voyeuristic—to watch and hear his sentences move, to follow them home. His synopsis, too, had truth's shape, its tapered drift. "A poor player sees finesses as opportunities. A good player views them as necessary evils. An expert player *treats* them as necessary evils."

Mimesis

Stan saw them making love through their half-closed curtain, and turned away. His instincts were frequently wrong, and Eric took the binoculars from him and adjusted the lens. Stan then saw a chance to score points with Noreen, by pointing out what he'd refused. Meanwhile Warren had borrowed Stan's camera and its zoom. Down two. "Why would anyone want to spy on anyone else?" Stan asked. Noreen merely smiled, waiting her turn. It was clear that Stan had confused an opportunity with an evil. The smarter ones instantly knew it mustn't be missed. The smartest knew it wasn't necessary, but a treat nonetheless.

· · ·

Outlaw

. . .

A word with romance behind it; if he thinks of himself so
named he can almost believe he's not a thug. He rides into
town unnoticed, in a car these days. The law is the instrument of restriction he's habituated himself to disturb. As he
sees it, the law would have a bull stop at red. It would reward
the safe, those who wait—even when nothing's coming—for
the light to change. The outlaw likes to elevate himself like
this. He imagines songs sung about him, years after his death.
Who alive, he thinks, is more alert than an outlaw? Who
better knows where he is and what it takes to live another
day? His definition of crime: a poor person's way of entering
into his own rights. But he's only seen half the movie, remembered only the get-aways and the easy girls. He's the
mistake he will make, which is why he can't see it. We would
cry out and warn him, but our roles in the ancient dramas are
fixed too.

Citizen

Robespierre was called one. Lenin preferred "comrade."
Kane of course was a citizen like Trump, only ironically one
of us. People who follow an abstraction all the way to its
deadly end or, like Trump, discover a curious sense of civics
by buying and erecting, need different designations. While
they reinvent the world, they'd like us to be obedient, responsible, maybe just quarrelsome enough to ask for clarifi-
cation. Many nights you and I watch TV, and I keep my hand
between your legs just for solace. I am the citizen of your
warm and wet places, and you—oh I would not speak for
you. "It's a far far better thing that I do," said one famous fic-
tive citizen, then did what he had to. And those of us who
think ourselves citizens of nowhere, or—almost the same—
citizens of the world, what do we do when our country calls?
"I ain't got nothing against them Congs," Ali said, always
defining himself, and some citizens loved him and others
were happy he wasn't allowed to punch anyone for years.

. . .

Strangers

. . .

The door opened. "I've come all the way from Telluride," the man said, holding something behind his back. He was middle-aged, conventionally dressed. "I've come all the way from Telluride because I heard you were doing poetry here." Here was Utah, a summer workshop, several of us seated around a seminar table. I was at its head. The man hadn't moved from the door. More quietly now, almost in a whisper, he again said where he'd come from, and asked if we could look at his poems. "Sorry," I said, "but we're in the middle of a class. I'm afraid we cannot." His right hand was still behind his back. "I'm very sorry to have bothered you," he said, "but I've come a long way." As he turned to leave, we could see several sheets of paper, presumably poems. When he was gone, a woman in class asked how I could have said that to him, she was sure he had a gun. The rest of the class, agitated, all talking at once, agreed. But I had never thought of a gun. I was sure he was concealing poems and, like many of the participants, had come from some distance for reasons literary and therefore personal to see how he might fare in this world.

Acquaintances

Not friends. A friend, after all, is someone with whom you need not discuss important subjects, though often you do. Nor do you have to clarify the status of your relationship, except when you must. Your good news doesn't bother him too much. Bad news brings out the empathetic best in you both. And each of you knows what small misfortunes to keep to yourself. To be just an acquaintance is normal enough. But terrible to be an acquaintance when you want to be a friend. Terrible when one person is thinking *friend*, the other *acquaintance*, and, after a long separation, those rapid, uncomfortable pats on the back when they hug. Show me a back patter, and I'll show you an acquaintance lost among his intuitions, whose body's Morse code is doubt, doubt, doubt. At a party full of acquaintances, it's almost as bad. What do we say after we've said what we usually say? Better to be a stranger with small hopes and a plan.

. . .

Suicides

. . .

It's usually a flirtation with Plath or Sexton or Berryman, but of my many students who've written about suicide, two have actually done it. After the second, years ago, I decided never to try to improve such a poem. We discuss it privately. I say, Don't do it. I say, Make an appointment with a counselor. Meanwhile, for myself, I've thought: how sensible. When my body becomes someone else's chore, when the mind fogs and the days lengthen and I'm unable to transform suffering into one of the higher pleasures, I hope to have the courage. Isn't there a curious elegance in how one moment passes into another? And won't it be easy to assume I'm dead already? But say a wise nurse, sensing my mood, shows me the tattoo on her breast. And a wise friend reminds me that the right solution is rarely the only one. I can imagine the lovely tactics of those who care. Rehearsals, postponements.

Funerals

No right way to feel. Pure grief perhaps if the death was sudden and your child's. But if a parent is lying there and you're no longer a child, likely that sadness is mixing with relief. Perhaps there's even a small corner of freedom, in which you find yourself making plans. When my brother wept at grandmother's funeral, I drifted back to when Anthony Salvo hit him with a rock. "I'll get you dickface, I'll get you dickface," he kept repeating through his tears. Once I caught myself thinking about baseball. Another time, as the coffin was lowered, I recalled that a group of larks is called an *exaltation*. And who hasn't imagined his own dark day, even his own eulogy, and what friend might deliver it, and the exact quavering of his voice.

. . .

Anger

. . .

A good thing, the experts say, the getting it out. I know
they're right. The few big times I've exhibited it, I felt spent
and righteously clean. A grudge is more my style, weeks,
months of resentment silently borne. At my worst, after
quarrels, I've kept it in and let it mix with any old bitterness
it could find. When it finally emerged—stunted, timed, cru-
elly calm—I was no one's decent man. But I'm seldom at my
worst and can only envy the brilliantly angry in books and in
films. I can't bear anyone routinely angry, anyone with a
childhood untamed. In truth, I prefer the manners of those
who keep most things to themselves. We're unable to enter-
tain opposites when we're angry. We're so bloody dull.
Everything I love about the mind disappears. I choose my
friends by the quality of their hesitations, their ability to be
ambivalent about the smallest things. Harm anyone I love,
though, and I'll seek you out and break you fucking in two.
I'd at least want to. I'd certainly understand anyone who
would.

Generosity

Not to be confused with philanthropy, capitalism's managed
leftovers. Or with largesse, a little something off the top.
Generosity is that palpable extra that comes along with the
gift, motiveless as a good wind. Best is the extra that comes
unencumbered: pure generosity of spirit, always replenishing
itself. We the less generous are quick to suspect it, remem-
bering what we've given and why. But those who have it ir-
radiate the day. They redefine the meaning of wealth. We fall
in love with them, we try to shine that brightly, yet before
long they've mostly instructed us about what it is we want to
keep. Blessed are the generous who keep enough for themselves so we can live with them without guilt. Blessed, too,
are those who receive well, so the generous get their reward.
A cold heart is not generosity's natural enemy. Scarcity is, and
its crucible as well. Blessed are the poor who give to the poor.
In our world of plenty when our daughter was three, at first
we laughed at her mistake: "Share, share, and like." Then we
praised it.

. . .

II

. . .

Sky

. . .

Sky seemed the most efficient and arrogant of words, one syllable for all of that. Sky, I'd think, and would reach for an adjective. Blue or gray, if I wasn't reaching hard. Or if I'd been asleep at sunrise, or come sunset dulled by habit or drink. Sometimes, though, blue or gray was exact—the way words of uninteresting people are sometimes true, but don't seem to matter. I despised those who'd see an azure sky. I couldn't speak to anyone inclined toward cerulean. Sky. Was there ever a noun that did so much work by itself? Clouds & sun & moon were its rightful properties, & high-flying birds, & every kind of weather. But it seemed reasonable to doubt that the sky was the limit. Heaven quaintly existed in some of our minds, which remained worried by how bodies wither, disappear. Yet many times now, I'd flown above the clouds and could report only the usual magnificence. Everyone would concur—even the skeptical had seen that world—and I knew I had offered nothing and must find other attitudes, other words.

Weather

It had its own channel now, like rock music. But it was more like an old, fixed drama whose characters play out their tendencies, which nevertheless startles us every time. Weather's perversities were legend. Tornadoes fond of mobile homes. The excesses of rain, and those prolonged withholdings. The sky, it could be said, was the stage, the director never present, the author deeply dead for centuries. Good weather almost kept us from despair, unless we lived where the sunny days disappeared into each other and words like "self-actualized" could be heard in neighborhoods removed from migrant labor and gangs. Snow was my favorite weather, linking the treacherous and the beautiful. I trusted snow cultures above all others—shared severity bringing out good will without an irritating imperative toward fairness. It was wrong, I decided, to make plans based on forecasts. It would be like consulting an oracle long after we learned that oracles never lived anyplace but in us, knowing how mistaken we've been and how suddenly our lives—without reason—have taken a turn for the better or the worse.

. . .

Bedroom

. . .

The submerged, the encoded—so much in dreams has happened separately to them there. The room itself, L-shaped. The bed, king-sized. On one wall a painting of two dancers—faceless, stylized poseurs. From floor to ceiling a bookcase holding experience imagined, distilled, sold and bought. The man's robe hanging from the end of a curtain rod. The woman's from a hook in the closet. Clutter is a word she uses. A bedroom should have none of it, she says. They argue often about this, their bedroom a compromise, her Japanese/Swedish modern sense of space and line, his accumulation of what's his, stretched to the delicacies of tolerance. Sex? They would have us assume, not unlike others, they've sought to blur the differences between the vulgar and the sublime, and that everything along the way, certainly the routine, has occurred. The walls are plaster and white. On the night table, a black phone and its answering machine next to a small, ordinary clock.

Kitchen

At first, the politics of it made sense to her. Now everything in the kitchen is his. The pans hanging from the wooden beam. The pots in the lower cupboard. The ladles, the tongs, the exact and various knives, the spices in the Lazy Susan, the recipes he's marked with grades A through F in his enormous file. His apron is his artist's smock. He's become so good his sense of good is changed for good. On a shelf the crockery he's collected from a dozen countries, functional and elegant. That new one, ochre with specks of blue, perfectly deep—all day he's been looking at it, thinking: *bouillabaisse*. Fennel, saffron, and just enough garlic to make the meal an aromatic visit to where gifted gypsies live on the edge of a slum. She used to cook, but now—in a kind of estrangement—has only to eat. She no longer shops. It's fun, he says, choosing the way a week will taste. The kitchen turns away from her when she walks in. The oven frowns. Only the refrigerator lets her in without grief, yet even in it she imagines places that have essentially become his now to reach.

· · ·

Landscapes

. . .

Never, for me, just mountains or clearings, or even these reedy marshes with egrets and herons amid the billboards. I need to put people in. Maybe I don't trust my eye, or the fact that there's an invisible person in every landscape, an inevitable imposition of mind. I want something adulterous to happen in the arboretum near the cove. I want the sound of a human voice to disturb the lily pond, perhaps someone explaining himself. No doubt also impositions of mind, though conscious, willful. Once in Minnesota, a newcomer, I was startled by the darkness of the soil as I drove from Worthington to Marshall. Cornfields recently plowed. I didn't quite know what I was seeing. "What's that?" I asked my companion. "That's dirt," he said. If only I'd been able to keep my mouth shut, trusting that I'd come back later to see it for what it was, then make it more identifiably mine. Maybe add a farmer. Have him walking in his dirt, say, up to his ankles, without worry or particular pride.

Interiors

In New Orleans, a Bed and Breakfast in a seamy part of town. Dentist's chair the seat of honor in the living room. Dark, the drapes closed, a lamp's three-way bulb clicked just once. I'm inside someone's version of inside. All the guests looking like they belong. Muffled hilarity coming from one of the other rooms. Paintings everywhere, on the walls, the floor. Painted by the proprietress who, on the side, reads the Tarot. In her long black gown she doesn't mind telling me things look rather dismal. Something about the Queen of Swords and the Hanged Man. I wake early the next morning for a flight. 5 A.M. She's sitting in the dentist's chair, reading a book about the end of the century. Says a man like me needs a proper breakfast. Wants to know everything I dreamed. *This*, I tell her, I think I dreamed this.

. . .

Fog

. . .

Above the lake, a whiteness. The water itself white, not a hint of gray or blue. The mountains invisible in the distance. Everything that had been clearly observed—suddenly a matter of trust. The luminosity of absence. Almost a sullen glow. We woke to it; we had not dreamed it in. It pressed against the windows, so we opened them. In its honor, we lay on the white sheets and made love. A part of it then, in its silky grasp, we touched in order not to disappear. We used each other as evidence of where we were. Soon the sun began its slow burn. The fog pinked. A little of what others call life— the conspicuous, the rosy—made its presence felt.

Luminescence

Not passion's sweaty radiance, or tantrum's righteous sheen. As far from incandescence as Garbo from Loren. Rather, a faraway kind of shining, a low temperature effect. The cold light of intelligence, sometimes. Stars and moon, of course, which inspire but don't burn. A meadow of fireflies, all those little seekers trying to find the opposite sex in the dark. The female flashes, the male flashes back. Exactly two seconds, and she'll respond again. An evening of connections. A dazzling luminescent calm. At another time, I'd favor fire's gorgeous predatory flame, shape-shifting as it moves, creating its own terms.

. . .

Natives

. . .

A neighbor—who makes it not his business, but his passion
to know the names of things—walked me through my property, naming everything that grew. He knew I was someone
who called a maple a tree, a marigold a flower. Deficiencies,
for sure. Four acres: the walk cut deeply into an afternoon. I
was grateful and a little bored. Before I got back to the house,
names blurred into names. But it was a loving thing that he
did, as I've come to understand his love. Part giving, part
showing off, an exuberance of motives, not always shared.
Rhododendron, goat rue, white pine. He pointed these out.
They're not yet mine. I say them now like someone who
loves song more than fact, inflection more than song.

Lovers

They come to the strange city where all signs are in a language they've failed to learn. Because they're in love, however, cars stop for them when they step into danger. Waiters bring them appetizers in seven different languages, which they sample without utensils, then suck each other's fingers clean. The waiters rush home to make love to their wives. The chambermaid in their hotel has been dreaming them back, has left mints and extra towels. They can feel that strange tug. But they've learned their urgencies are sweeter the more they're delayed. It is April. They buy identical dark blue berets, and stroll by the river where at dusk even people who dislike each other walk arm in arm. Among them they feel disguised, though it's obvious to everyone that they come from a country that exists for only moments at a time.

. . .

Music

. . .

Something overheard from the dissonant street—a screech, a bang—taken in and arranged. A subjective correlative. Sequences, resolutions, deliberate unfulfillments. The sublimity of large and small moments surrendering to the whole. What feeling feels like over time. An attempt to screw up what feeling feels like over time. Heartbreak and a high C. The twang the nervous system wants when it's in revolt. The often welcome melodic lie. Ululation and a stomp of heels, scat-sense, voice and ear living together in brilliant sin. The soul's undersong. The orchestration of randomness, a flirtation with the boundaries of silence and space. When Bun-Ching played last night—a reminder that the self wants to disappear, be taken away from itself and returned.

Noise

Solitude unchosen; the drone of it rising to a buzz. That poet you hate, his dead tune on a bad instrument. Hungover, the terrible fork glancing the excruciating plate and—that same morning—the frisson of corduroy, your own, as you walk. Loud music, not yours; somebody else's good time. The oratory of an enemy. The cacophony of someone asking for love. Another remark after the argument's been conceded, or the story's over. Your stupid, habitual politeness when the telemarketer calls. The restrained ha-ha when only a belly laugh will honor the moment. Any complaint, even the gentlest, from a person incapable of praise. Someone you know you'll not see again—the dull click of an unslammed door.

. . .

Flirtation

. . .

In a corner at the cafe. Two of them because it takes two. All parry now, no thrust. The waiters know how to leave them alone. Outside, waiting to be seated: Illness, Boredom, Sorrow. As sure of themselves as ever. Loneliness already seated, dining with a group. For the man and woman, not much of an investment yet. Their currency disposable: hope & charm. Layers of it before the heart will be exposed. Their souls, at this stage, not in the vicinity. A tilt of the head, the puffing up, this little dance—they could be goats or birds. Too soon to be a story, just sequences. The future occurring. The eros of moving into it while keeping it at bay. The weight of survival, the daily trivia, all suspended. Between them, the unknown almost palpable now. Look, Sorrow's just been let in and given its favorite table at the far end of the room. It's taking off its cloak. They'll not see it for a while.

Revision

A friend of mine woke early one morning, made breakfast for himself and, while looking out his back window, realized for the first time how much he hated his yard. In fact, he was overwhelmed by how ordinary it was. His wife of fourteen years was still asleep. He left before she woke, and from his office called a landscaper, indicating what he wanted—a garden, a small waterfall; all the rest would be left to the landscaper's sense of design. When the landscaper and his men arrived the next day, my friend's wife greeted them and showed them the yard. She was pleased by what her husband had initiated. Over the phone, the landscaper told my friend: $10,000. Go ahead, he said. The job took two weeks, and by the end the yard was stunning, a half acre of paths and hedges and, yes, a flower garden and a little waterfall over which a bridge had been constructed. It was finished on a Tuesday. He remembers precisely because that was the day he told her he was leaving. He had no place to go and nobody waiting for him, but—he was very sorry—he felt they must separate.

．．．

Faces

. . .

High school reunions are the proving grounds. Say, one's twenty-fifth. So interesting to see how character can overcome bone structure. Pretty, handsome, cute—how those attributes, those intimidations, once seemed permanent. No need to mark the many ways faces go bad. Or the sadness, for example, of remaining cute. Time is good only to those who survive its accidents, who manage to befriend it. Yet what advantages they have, the ones who start so well. They are the panthers and leopards created by an unjust god and allowed to move among the hyenas and goats. Sometimes, at any rate. We never knew how intelligence could insinuate its way into eyes and mouth, could become a kind of glamor. We never knew one could grow a face. Still, at every reunion there are a few whose beauty has deepened, sculpted by experience into a new place of consideration in our revised dreams. Barbara. Oh, I still wouldn't approach her, still wouldn't dial whatever her number had become.

Bodies

The good zoo of them, the names we could name them if we
dared to begin! The musclebound go-away-from-me. The
fleshy invite-me-in. We sit for hours in springtime and watch
them pass. Only some do we undress, though we can't help
but invent a life for each. We can almost tell by their walk
and their arms' degree of swing how they might be in bed.
We intuit those bodies we'd be impelled to obey, and bodies
that would be at the mercy of ours, and bodies so kindred
that all leverage would disappear. In the dark, they often curl
into question marks. We love the ones that ease us beyond
unease. Some, of course, are originals, seem connected to
their own universe, their own first cause. Only the arrogant
among us take credit for making them respond. And mine?
Difficult, after a while, to love one's own—its inconsistencies,
the classic diminutions, the terror of having only one. But if
bodies had epitaphs, I'd want mine to read: *It rattled its cage.
It wouldn't be appeased.*

. . .

Clothing: Men

. . .

In business, years ago, I dressed to get ahead, my gray suit
saying, "I'm one of you, and kill sometimes when I don't
need to eat, I understand the rules." The fop in graphics envied women their scarves and hues. I thought he'd mistaken
his century, or was this one's deliberate fool. I know now,
like most of us, he dressed to be properly found. Now the
white teenager in the neighborhood turns his cap backwards,
just catching on, and already his black counterpart's pants
are lower than anyone's ever seen. It's palpable, his alien-
ation; no doubt he'll keep inventing the uniform. What
lengths of embellishment we'll go to say who we are! So it is,
with someone new, when for love or sex we strip down to our
skins, that we're suddenly almost no one at all. Some of us
are dangerous then, without our leather and chains. Unmade
men, we must hope—for the woman's sake—that our moth-
ers were mostly kind to us and held us and dressed us warmly
for the snow.

Clothing: Women

An entire day at stake: the high school girl's choice of soft
sweater or propriety's white blouse. Or the executive's perfectly undisturbing boardroom suit in her closet next to some
good-trouble she'll wear when she wants. It's a sexual deci-
sion not to be sexual, for her at least. Unlike a man, so many
latitudes of display. Women understand early what all artists
know: artifice can lead to the genuine. Even the woman
known for her apron sometimes slips out out of it into another world, a world made possible because she put on its
clothes. Mix 'n Match. A spiked belt and sensible shoes. Jeans
and decolletage. Options, or why not, that ordinary cotton
print mixed with nothing but herself. I've marvelled at them
all. The woman who every day wears only her politics. The
gum chewer and that tank top stuck to her like an attitude. I
watch them walking on the boulevard, their guises and dis-
guises signalling: come close, stay away, or I'm not thinking
of you at all.

. . .

Midnight

. . .

'Round midnight. At some midnight place. The preludes to
sex or loneliness nearing their end. Soon the actual, the *or* removed, the mix. Midnight was once, for me, a kind of beginning. I burned its available oil. For years it retained its old
curfew time's dark appeal. Now I think of bars getting nasty
and maudlin. My friend the insomniac trying another position, still pressing. The Blue Diamond diner near the college
starting to hum. I'm probably asleep, part of me waiting for
that screech owl and its nightly screech. I've flossed and
brushed, I've taken some pills that keep me even in the race
I'll lose. Those nuanced silences, a house's late-night tics—I
miss them. I miss the way I used to visit myself. But midnight
has always belonged to those of us who would not stop at it,
who thought, if we were thinking at all at that hour, something which could not come at noon would certainly come.
Certainly: I used to use that word back then.

Noon

Lovers in hotel rooms having their sweet hour, and when
they emerge the noon sun a son-of-a-bitch, all scrutiny, no
slack. Or we walk out of our businesses into it and the
schmooze of a lunch. Or, as I remember in Cottonwood, the
whistle blows. The grain elevator man and Merle from the
hardware store lunch at home. Or, in a more distant life,
Frankie Mauro the halfback opens his brown bag and says,
"Goddammit, peanut butter and jelly again!" and when we
wonder why he hasn't asked his mother to make him something else, he says he makes it himself. Noon is like that, the
comedy of too much out front, the analysand thinking he's
telling the truth when he says what he feels, Frankie Mauro
missing—in front of all of us—his own joke. It's gossip's hour,
a bad time for tears. It's already too late for the elusive the-
orem to be solved. In lousy jobs, it's toward what the morning leans. It's around the time the nightwatchman taps the
other side of his bed, and no one's there. And the profligate,
too, are just waking then, scented with the night, seeming
lucky to all of us who don't know them well.

. . .

Legacy

. . .

Hell's Kitchen Irish Catholic. German Jew from Boston. Scotch protestant down from Prince Edward Island. Dunn, Fleischman, MacKenzie—they're all the ancestry I know, except for my mother, a mixed breed, Fleischman/MacKenzie, American as a good dream. My father a salesman. Grandfather: merchant marine turned theatrical agent. Both talkers, storytellers, a drinking man and a flesh man. Early on, the women upper West Side-stylish, then housewives housebound, generous in their generation's shackles. All of us in the same house, Jewish part of Forest Hills; a lone Italian on our block and my brother and me: The Gentiles. Catechism, First Communion, Confirmation, the taking of an extra middle name—Francis—in honor of my father. Yet among the motley, no orthodoxy possible. Mere gestures by each of us toward the various pieties. Then my father's gamble and failure, his boozy solution. Grandfather's betrayal. Every sad thing they did complicated by their decency, and nobody but me privy to the secret truths. And yet mine was the childhood my friends envied. An open door, cookies. No public grief or grievances. Everything taken in, lived with.

Silence

Over the years, I've spoken too much about it.

. . .

Information

. . .

Soon we'll want less of it. Like blood-slowed mosquitoes, we'll try to become unwebbed, free of what bloats and keeps us. How good it will be to pronounce synecdoche all over the country, seek the quintessential, not listen to a speech or treatise that is additive. Will an old hunger for poetry be re-suscitated—poetry, not just the slam of our voices? Might the many suddenly understand how the dashes in Dickin-son's poems are simultaneously a function of speed and delay, which will feel personal to them, directive? I see us wanting to move in our lives as she did in poems—swiftness of ob-servation to insight, yes, but a little hesitation too, a smart foot on the brake all the way up the dangerous Highway. Then an old sense of the sufficient: enough history to avoid becoming history, enough of the present to be clear-headed, sharp-eyed, assassins of the extra.

Personal

I'm frequently overwhelmed by the monotony of a typical day. Like most people, I pretend not to be excited by catastrophes. I prefer a life that won't cohere, that scrutiny might destroy, to a life the populace might approve of. To my fellow prisoners I say, Just because the escape tunnel goes on forever is no reason to stop digging. Because I've often felt what I've said, I know that nobody's problem was ever solved by feeling deeply about it. I've said the opposite of this, and stand by what I said. I am a pagan and enjoy a pagan's tragic optimism. I'll dance to almost anything, however awful, if the beat is good. I know several consolations for the letdowns and sorrows of experience, but intend to keep them to myself. Every secret I've ever told concealed another secret. I prefer relationships in which so little is asked of me I feel free enough to be generous.

. . .

Frivolity

· · ·

Two cannibals were eating a clown, and one said to the other, "Does this taste funny to you?" I said this as I was passing the corn, and a familiar contagion began. Someone else said his high school student wrote that she had "no self of steam." And because we were all teachers this was followed by "We all had something up our selves" and "Because I was an incredibly large feminist, I agreed with everything she said"—some of our sad pleasures. Then the most dignified person at the table, a woman, told a long joke about a bear who keeps sneaking up on the hunter who pursues it, and each time fucks him up the ass. It was hilarious long before she reached the punchline, such a bad joke that no vulgarian could possibly tell it well. There was a long silence, no one for a while able to think of anything in the going spirit, or gauche enough to say something straight. I remembered a recent paper that contained, "Joyce's narrator lived in an uninhibited two-story house," and the table was off again. Everyone trusting everyone else's seriousness.

Seriousness

Driving the Garden State Parkway to New York, I pointed
out two crows to a woman who believed crows always travel
in threes. And later just one crow eating the carcass of a
squirrel. "The others are nearby," she said, "hidden in trees."
She was sure. Now and then she'd say "See!" and a clear dark
trinity of crows would be standing on the grass. I told her she
was wrong to under- or overestimate crows, and wondered
out loud if three crows together made any evolutionary
sense. I was almost getting serious now. Near Forked River
we saw five. "There's three," she said, "and two others with
a friend in a tree." I looked to see if she was smiling. She
wasn't. Or she was. "Men like you," she said, "need it written down, notarized, and signed."

. . .

Reading

. . .

From his hotel balcony in Italy he sees a lovely woman sunning herself on the balcony adjacent to his. Only a little wall and a few large plants separate them. She's topless, but after a while that doesn't matter. She's reading a book he's written, and he can see her lips moving to some of his words. When she wets thumb and index finger to turn a page he almost gasps. Never has silence served him so well. The woman, he concludes, knows that he's watching her. Too much of a coincidence otherwise. But the fact is—he'll learn this later— she doesn't know. She adjusts the lounge chair and turns to lie on her stomach. Her breasts press into the obliging cushion. The book is open and she's propped herself on her elbows, smiling at something he's written. "What is pleasing you?" he's tempted to ask, but chooses instead to imagine it's the scene in which the protagonist feels she's a prisoner of her own taste. He retreats to his room, packs, unpacks, then writes a note, which he carries to the concierge. "For the woman in Room 408" it says, and he begins to worry about the disappointments of the actual.

Erasure

I've crossed things out with a thin, single stroke so the original could be read, leaving for investigation both correction and the corrected. I've intentionally erased two people from my life, only two, yet can't help following the traces of them. Like pentimento, some old marks, some ruins, ghosting my days and nights. Any fictionist knows that one event, even if poorly executed, can make another happen, the slightest authenticity creating a path to the hidden. One way to revise: erase something, erase something else, see what's left standing, then decide if it deserves companions. Total erasure makes sense too, a grand cleaning up after the misconceived party, a starting over with a better nothing. The eros of beginnings! Yet even then, who doesn't desire to leave a trail, barely followable, or dream of being properly found by someone who might exquisitely look and care?

. . .

III

. . .

Reflection

. . .

A mirror is the beginning of a comedy, and comedies, like the truth, are always a little cruel. But it isn't true that mirrors never lie. They lack attitude, and therefore cannot be wholly trusted. A hangover means as much to them as a great sadness. Sometimes we can hardly recognize ourselves in a mirror—because the image is so accurate. We understand the need to shatter, to transmogrify, in order to feel more like ourselves. If we place a bowl in front of a mirror, it is an arrangement so artificial that what's real—the bowl, the mirror, and the viewing eye—constitute a separate reality. Good realism is like that. The inanimate especially longs to be rescued by viewpoint more than by passion or conviction.

Shadow

A shadow makes us think twice, thus we link it with doubt and worry. Something has gotten in the way, and it's often us. We elongate, flatten. At a streetcorner, we can be seen before we arrive. The truth, a shadow implies, is in perspective, a matter of what's behind us. The natural is merely one possibility; artificial light serves just fine. In either case, concealment is a part of clarity. A shadow, like some of us, is always a citizen of where it finds itself. Pavement. Hardwood floor. It finds its texture as it goes. In this way it is more palpable, say, than a woman unseen except by her mirror. Or a solitary man, the keyhole to his sunlit room closed-up with a key. Yet I long for anyone with a shadowy past, half texture-in-the-making, half half-told-story, a sweet balance between style and disclosure.

. . .

Experts

· · ·

The Old Lady Moth hides by day in the porch of a house, or behind curtains. Less of a homebody, the Leopard Moth rests on tree trunks. And it's said that the Red-Tipped Flower Beetle, when disturbed, produces two pairs of scarlet, bladderlike organs, the function of which is not known. All of which means that the smallest things have their observers, that if you exist, you might be someone's life work. It's all language and personality after that, or so it seems. We can imagine the pleasure the Common Dung Fly expert took in saying that it frequents flowers for nectar, but during dull periods will sit on herbage near dung pats and attack other flies, cutting the nerve cords of their necks with its well-developed teeth, then sucking their juices. We're told the dragonfly that outflies and outmaneuvers smaller dragonflies is called The Emperor. Aphids suck the sap of plants, said someone who loved esses. I'm of course in a library, where experts have been gathered to delineate and disagree. A meteorologist asserts matter-of-factly that each day is a mystery story. A painter writes: I mark, stain, trespass.

Ignorance

In Pennsylvania, among some mountain people, ignorant means rude. They also say backward when we would say shy. They are ignorant of our parlance, but they're not rude, maybe just a little backward in our sense of the word. Surely someone, some farmer or musician or mechanic, is thinking the same about us. Bliss? No. What we don't know chains us, leaves us sitting in the valley with a stupid smile. We discover our ignorance as we go. After a lifetime, if we've been attentive, we should fall to our knees before the vastness, the ungraspable minutiae of our world. We should suspect that it constitutes our God. And we so-called experts of this or that, could we have done more than play our one chord? Wisdom is to know, at best, that we make only a little good noise, a few small dents. It's why the wise laugh a lot, why the laughter of metaphysicians echoes in the spaces they probe. We walk out of our houses into the enormity of our task. What kind of ant is that? Who named the phlox? Is that a path or a rut?

. . .

Emblems

. . .

It's nearing its end, our century of acquisition and dazzle,
the quick score, the panache of images researched to deceive.
So I say no more the peacock's solo fashion show and its
screech of pride. No more the eagle or hawk, those paragons
with their good eyes for small prey and their superior flight.
As emblems, let them be dead the way a doornail is dead as
a comparison for dead. The way a mouse no longer invites us
to consider how quiet quiet is. For the next century, I rec-
ommend the auk and the grebe. Heavy bird with small wings,
inefficient flyer, the auk uses its wings to swim underwater.
Its chest therefore is enormous. It can hold its breath brilliantly until it accomplishes what it needs. I say our culture
needs the auk on stamps, on posters in the rooms of shy children who like to read and take in. And we also need the
grebe, foot-propelled diving bird with no known relative,
fossil or modern. Inspiring and mysterious that it flies chiefly
at night, especially by moonlight, and by day keeps a regular
job at the shore. Let's name a team after it, or a school.

Heroes

Once we welcomed the anti-, the un-. We debunked who-
ever was in the top bunk, tore down what wouldn't stand up.
It was just another romance, of course, Belmondo instead of
Odysseus, as if the attainable with a cigarette in its mouth was
a new destiny, as if heroes should resemble us. But I admired
Bill Russell the basketball player, and Jean Paul Sartre his
apartment apart from de Beauvoir and, like Russell, how he
looked difficulty in its dark, persistent eye. I choked up at re-
plays of Welsh saying to McCarthy, "Have you no decency,
sir?" I wanted to speak like Churchill if things were to get
grim. And now when young people are asked about their heroes, they get more silent than a mouse on tiptoe, or cite
some rock star or Billy Graham, or, touchingly, their parents.
There's nothing high up for them that scrutiny hasn't
brought down. Heroes need a moment or two slowed into
memory, stopped, emblazoned. They need to be caught
swimming underwater for miles when the sky has gotten
crowded with lies. We must not ask what they do in their
spare time, or about their failures at love, or the money they
took from that till when they were young. Their job is to go
further and deeper than we dare. *If only*, we should find ourselves thinking. *What if* . . .

. . .

Scapegoat

. . .

It's the Day of Atonement, and Aaron has a brilliant idea. Two goats as offerings to the Lord. One he kills as a personal atonement for himself and his house. The other is the scapegoat. He lays both hands on its head, confessing the sins of the people, then sends it off into the wilderness. Poor goats. Lucky, unburdened people. It's easy to see why such an idea caught on. There's a burnt offering too, involving a ram; in the face of the ineffable, Aaron tries to cover all bases. But we're most interested in the goat that bears our large and small mistakes, and carries them away from us. Leviticus knew how to tell a story, but here's what was never reported: The Lord saw the goat in the wilderness, stumbling, half-dead. He said to it: A goat's life is an awful thing. This was not My intention. What they've done to you is just one more of their sins.

Criminal

Born wrong. Could be as simple as that. Wrong parents. Wrong country. Or born anywhere, eminently decent, but on the wrong side of a bad law. Then there's the luck that separates forgotten incident from criminal one, like the time I accidentally set the corner lot ablaze, a nasty wind that day, no witnesses. I think too of the children I might have killed had they timed their carelessness just right, a trace of liquor on my breath, their ball rolling into the street, my car going slightly faster than slow. Fingerprinted. Front-paged. Instead, a normal evening at home, a citizen, nearly upright. Aren't most of us, caught or not, responsible for some kind of choice? And of course certain criminals calculate, plan, hide in the bushes, alter the books. So little separates me from them. Send us off into the wilderness without a goat, bearing our own burdens. Or maybe we deserve worse, or just to be left alone? We probably have more than one destiny, but one of them for sure is to meet up with ourselves, no Lord, no one to condemn or forgive.

· · ·

Hegemony

. . .

For many, hurt has its own ethics, a burning cheek that insists the slap be returned. Not a matter of honor, but of justice. Honor is a word the powerful often invoke when they wish the order that serves them to stay the same. Keep silent, own up—it all depends on who needs to be protected. Never shoot a man in the back—the code of someone whose home hasn't been broken into, or country invaded. Let's not be honorable when the rules aren't ours, the disenfranchised conclude. The rebels among them add, For the sake of a great cause, who wouldn't betray a lesser cause, or lie about anything large or small? In the face of deprivation, the manners that honor breeds can be obscene. And yet when such honor is defeated, shown for what it is, isn't he an unwise victor who doesn't replace it with a version of his own?

Honor

Shouldn't we forgive in others what we ourselves have done, or might do? Difficult, agonizing. Yet a matter of honor for some of us. I remember being startled by a woman saying to me that honor was a man's term. I didn't know what she meant. Character, I'd always believed, should transcend what psychology would excuse. She meant that grievances contain certain permissions. How many? I wanted to say. Aren't we also known by what we won't do? To her I was using a language I was privileged to use. Perhaps. But many of us have been wronged. And after we take our revenge, what do we do when the moral balance shifts to our side? Many of us, too, are pigs, I should have said, and don't figure in matters of honor. Pigs—though real pigs deserve a better name— want only to extend their advantages. The women I admire know it would take all of their decency not to do the same.

. . .

Mercy

. . .

We infidels (though only those of us who've been caught)
lean toward its white light, its ability to see us with and beyond our faults. It's what we beg for, but seldom seem able to
bestow. The merciful spare; some even forgive. Yet sometimes they must have regarded some of us, and said *No*. They
must have invoked a word like *justice*, and turned away from
us, and spat. Thus the body's little fiesta when they lift the
noose from our necks, or when they give the wayward heart
one more earthly chance. And with each act they deepen
their power, for mercy comes from power and is one of its re-
wards. How good the merciful must feel! But can they know,
finally, how humiliating it is to be spared? Our accentuated
smallness. The coming months of obeisance and gratitude.

Vengeance

The sheer sensuousness of returning an offense. The release.
Then no place to go but back into ourselves where suddenly
we're cool and numb. That node of anger, that galvanizer,
gone. No excuse left to delay living our lives. Maybe only
love is as personal. The singularity, the intense focus. Once,
though, in existentialism's first grasp, I was content to believe
that in time the wicked would hang themselves. Nothing we
need do to them. I'd forgotten how hurt won't let philosophy
be king, that hurt wears its own crown, wants to rid itself of
itself. But so much of vengeance is a quiet affair. Just
vengeance and me, the cause elsewhere, perhaps in another
city, enjoying himself, untroubled by my trouble with him.
I've taken him to sleep with me where he's met his proper
death. No mercy in that dark realm. And no satisfaction
when I woke.

· · ·

Superstition

. . .

The crack in the sidewalk, and a broken back. The ladder under which a black cat must not stroll. Knock on wood. There are things we must ward off or forestall. Superstition is the irrationality we bring to the irrational world. It's a way of pressing back. Because science only takes us so far into the unseen order of things. Because even if we know why it rains we don't know if it will. The athlete crosses himself before a free throw. The shot goes in, and the Trinity made it happen. It misses: a mere failure of concentration. But sympathetic magic succeeds more often than it doesn't. We sweep popcorn off of the veranda to keep the elephants away. The elephants don't come! To keep the one you want you dig up a footprint of hers and put it in a flowerpot. She stays with you for months! This is how pagans pray. It's heaven when it works.

Certainty

Taxes have loopholes, but not even Heisenberg could make death uncertain. Certainty is what we feel when we know a little less than enough. It's only about uninteresting things that we can be wholly certain. This is a refrigerator, for example. Or that's a plum. If some philosophers want to worry about these designations, I'm quite certain a plum is a plum. If it were called, say, a trampoline, I'd know it was the same tasty thing. About matters of the heart only negative capability will do. About real time and imaginary time let the dreamer meet the physicist for a friendly duel. The world of intellect: inseparable from the world of feeling. That's a certainty. It's how it feels.

. . .

Irony

. . .

Yang Lian, poet in exile, said he didn't think there was a word for irony in Chinese. Earlier that day in the Italian Alps, he put "Beware of the dangerous animal" on his studio door because too many passersby were looking in. In the evening—deep-voiced, haunting—he chanted Mongolian love songs. Mild tales of courtship, deemed risqué, they were among the solaces the Cultural Revolution banned, beautiful as a Victorian woman's ankle must have been to a man deprived. Lian smiled as he described his past, and it was clear that irony manages the moment, won't let the world hurt us, that its strength is also its weakness. Yet it always winks and suggests. In "Brutus is an honorable man," we see it at its slyest. If Lian had said, "Mao was a prince," we would have heard irony's familiar lapse into sarcasm. But he was speaking of exile, home. The life of an ironist can begin even when two lesser things fracture and pull.

Earnestness

The whole truth and nothing but the truth. The mind not at
play, thus the earnest never tripping themselves into new
news, never dancing the surprising, incorrect dance. Victims
of the Important Subject and its static weight, not serious
enough to bear the tension of opposites or the comedy of
loose ends, they finish those sentences whose conclusions we
foresaw centuries ago. Yet we've been them. We've heard
ourselves drone on about our specialties, the things we're
sure others need to know. Still, earnestness has its place. As
with sincerity, its dull twin, it sometimes correctly buries our
dead, it takes us seriously when nothing less or more will do.
Nice to think, though, that in private the undertaker jokes
about the corpse. And that the psychologist—perhaps moments after we've left the room—wisecracks that his patients
never stop talking about themselves.

. . .

Ambition

. . .

No tribe to sing to, so we sing a difficult tune. The self with its dislocations, its absences, careening toward the extreme. Hungry for the approval of a few. Still, our work makes its own claims. What we've tried for, how close we've come, all there on the page. Especially what we haven't tried for—that failure of ambition. Those bad adjectives—blind, naked, unbridled—waiting for the desperate self looking to enlist others in its cause. But who among us doesn't want a prize and a place at the table? Who doesn't desire his best words to live in the world? Okay, but first we're interested in what is, and in how it feels. In constructing how it feels? In singing it true? The architecture of the song, the song in the mortar and brick—the inseparable is what we want. Then, maybe, what we want for ourselves.

Humility

Important to understand our true size in the universe. Thus if we spit in its indifferent meaningless eye, we know to spit high and with all our might. Small fits only some of us well. The humble size-down to slip in, never break a seam. They eat their undelicious pie at all hours of the day. Isn't humility best a sometimes thing? Stunned by someone else's grace or better mind, we pause; we learn and praise. Stunned by nature's ferocity, we go inside a while. But we come out! We make a few more claims about what we've seen and thought. Sure, arrogance is always nearby. Foolish to embrace it, or to entirely turn away. In fact we were sure we needed a little of its brashness, its disregard for popularity, if we were to have anything to say.

. . .

Hypocrisy

. . .

The hypocrite lacks the language of excusable hypocrisy, thus gets caught and named. He doesn't know how to finesse his discrepancies, his great gap between statements and deeds. And sometimes he's just hopeless, the problem so rooted in character he cannot be redeemed. We're worse than he, having learned the grease of manners, the smoke screens of style. When confronted with inconsistencies, we say we contain multitudes. Or admit to just enough sleaziness so we'll be thought of as complicitous, attractively perverse. Eventually, over a lifetime, we're found out, if not by others then harshly by ourselves. Yet hypocrisy is a social virtue. A day without it is likely to be a cruel day indeed. In public we say "How cute" about the ugly baby, yet can't help but note its ugliness when we get home. Privately we've laughed a few times at racial jokes, yet deplore racial jokes. Can we imagine a world without hyprocisy? Would we want to live in it? All that brutality trying to pass as honesty. Please say it behind my back.

Precision

On a gravestone: "For Andrew 1912–1935 who died saving his drowning brother." Under that: "The White Flower of a Blameless Life." And I remembered years ago hesitating on the shore as the tide took a screaming man out into the Northumberland Strait. A poor swimmer, I saved his life by summoning a fisherman who was docking a boat. Hero? Coward? Neither word seemed to fit. If he had drowned and I had drowned, one certainly can imagine different words, words with modifiers, for me. Cowardice has more to do with what we *can* do, and don't. Which makes most of us cowards, I suppose. It's a cousin to ambivalence, and why thinkers—we hesitators—are suspect in all popular art. Andrew, though, may have been a hero. But "The White Flower of a Blameless Life"? Please. Let's hope his loved ones simply were overwhelmed by grief.

. . .

Cynicism

. . .

Originally, for the Greek Cynics, an issue of virtue and self-control. Virtue was the only good; self-control the only means for attaining it. Easy to see that the word was off to a bad start. But in modern parlance, cynicism is a distrust of motives, an overriding suspicion of self-interest. The cynic, therefore, has the luxury of being mostly correct. Wilde had his number perfectly: "Someone who knows the price of everything and the value of nothing." What do we value? What do we love? A skeptic is no one's favorite lover, but I can't help think as a skeptic might. I love what's left after love has been tested. I value the doubt that gets the scientist to the solution. When a skeptic meets a cynic on the street: "Nice day, so far," the skeptic says. The cynic has to think about that.

Ego

The egoless: hard to trust they know what should be cherished and kept. The egotistical: they like too much—regardless of content—what is theirs. I admire Whitman's ego, capacious but not big. Shouldn't ego be cultivated until it's at least personality? Maybe then, as some have counseled, we could give it up, or keep it from getting in the way. Divestiture: Whitman's the model; something of him and what he accumulated and made. For us. There'll always be jibes from those who equate ego with a rampant, vainglorious I. There'll always be the cynics who make less of more. Let them have less. I say all this knowing many of us have selves divided. Fragments everywhere. At best a little cutting, a little paste.

· · ·

Advantages

. . .

Better to be an insect if you're going to fall. An ant is no more than a feather. A fly has its wings. And what an elegant form of support the daddy-longlegs has. So much bounce in the knees, or where knees should be. I've watched one fall from a height fifty times its size, and begin its strange walk. You can drop a mouse down a thousand-foot mine shaft—experts say it might survive. A rat would be killed, a man broken and killed. The ant, of course, can carry a huge crumb up a hill. But a wet ant will not get far. Wetness to an insect is worse than what Sisyphus was condemned to do. Compelled to lift many times its own weight, the fly struggles in our shower stalls and in a storm. In fact, an insect going for a drink is in as great danger as a man leaning out over a cliff in search of food. We have common sense to save us, at least some of us do. Insects have a proboscis, which works just as well. But isn't this the way it is? Small or big, one night we go out for an innocent spin and find ourselves, like the fly, in the suddenly bad neighborhood of a web, not one of our advantages the slightest bit good.

Superiority

A superior thing is its own testimony, like Notre Dame or a Porsche. Even standing still, the Porsche is evidence of a vanity so serious we don't accuse it of the showiness that is vanity's sin. I could be speaking about a well-made bowl or watch. Our advantage over perfect things is we can know many, while perfection only knows itself. And we have our failures, which can lead to reassessment and discretion and balance, those tools for bettering ourselves. Superior individuals, though, sometimes appear to have given birth to themselves, and move through their world like fine cars on a crowded road. Others declare who they are. Everything they've thought and done seems folded deeply into everything they aspire to be. I've known one or two. When they broke down, it seemed they should have been able to fix themselves.

. . .

Anonymity

. . .

Of poets, there's Anonymous, more famous than many who sign their names. Even the most famous American poet could walk down Fifth Avenue in sunlight and not be known. Few poets, therefore, or bus drivers or clerks, for that matter, seek anonymity. Why seek what is already yours? Anonymity suggests a chosen state, a series of remote, discrete, not necessarily unhappy days. It presumes you've done something noteworthy, that the voyeuristic public wants to breathe your air. Or you're a squealer, a rat, the government loves you, and your old bad friends are looking for a man you can't afford to be. Fame is death to you. To the unrecognized, the always-passed-over, fame seems like manna, and actually might be if they can keep from needing it. Better if it comes when you're older, friends already in place, character lines etched around your mouth and eyes. And there you are, almost safe, committed to the habits that have limited you for years.

Indifference

There's evidence of life in hatefulness, which is why indifference, not hate, is the opposite of love. Between lovers, what's worse than a shrug? Or you look in the mirror, and not even an old friend stares back, or anybody you'd be inclined to improve. Otherwise, indifference may be what you can't help feeling toward someone who can't help inspiring it. It can be as natural as a yawn, not necessarily a failing or a falling away. Justified or not, indifference is never anything to be proud of; there's not a situation it has ever made better. For those regulars of indifference, to whom so little matters, some synapse between brain and society has snapped, some link between hearts and other hearts. They are beyond hurt, these masters of distance, they don't permit themselves the sweetness of the tragic world.

. . .

Despair

. . .

How to stare meaninglessness in its large milky eye, and continue on? It's our tragic condition; if only he could accept it he might have a new kind of freedom. But all he can think of is a tautology: this meaninglessness is meaningless. He's no longer excited that the world is full of ice cream cones to be licked, fast cars to drive with women of various speeds, and words, so many words waiting to be used in the proper order. The oppressiveness of vitality! The man who despairs will have none of it. For him, hope is even more abstract than God, and the little cocoon he's built around himself offers a curious satisfaction. A firing squad is not coming in the morning. He just feels as if it is. His doctor is all pill and euphemism. Knock, knock. The Jehovah's Witnesses are at the door, three of them, cheerful beyond decency. They'd like to explain a few things.

Illness

A man learns he has an incurable illness, and for months will not or cannot speak its language. When he's not staring at the walls of his house, he's silent among friends. Then he gets on a plane and hums through the sky, eats his way through Paris, and hoo-hahs into Luxembourg with a tormented Belgian heiress he's met on a train. She instructs him, simply by being herself, about what it is he doesn't want. Around this time, he realizes he's behaving and speaking like a man who has an incurable illness, and returns to his wife, though she's been doing some hoo-hahing of her own and kisses him wrongly and for too long. It's a moment of perfect understanding, better than forgiveness, and each turns the other loose so that they might choose each other again. Meanwhile, in his absence, a wheelchair ramp has been built, he senses Debilitation planning a little party, the caterer at this very moment (he imagines) is wrapping prosciutto around fruit that feels nothing when the toothpick is inserted. He's reconciled to nothing. He calls it dancing, this soft-shoe he does, this dragging. That worsening tremor— that's the new way he's come to lead the band. It looks like passion.

· · ·

Insurance

. . .

When you insure your life it's a bet for your heirs, which
you win by dying. And a hedged bet for the big companies,
who've already invested your premiums in commodities and
futures. Kafka couldn't have invented it any better. When I
was 19, my father arranged a summer job for me with New
York Life. All I had to do was take the psychological test, and
I was in. "Do you ever have black, tarry bowel movements?"
one of the questions asked, and I wavered, sure my answer
would mean everything to New York Life. "Yes," I decided,
which couldn't have been the only reason I flunked. My father was disappointed and I ashamed. And now I think my
failure was a kind of insurance—the best I ever fell into—
against doing such work. Ever since, I've tried to live my life
so that living would be its own annuity, in its own time. A bet
in the dark, the beneficiaries always in doubt.

Luck

Years ago at Aqueduct, my friend Joe, a Marxist, bet on a
horse called Marxism in the third race. Its odds were 8 to 1,
which seemed about right. And it won. Eighteen bucks for a
two dollar bet; he didn't share it with the masses, you can be
sure. This is a true story about luck in the small. In the large,
he had bet on a horse that immediately thereafter seemed to
get old. Never won again. History's always a bad bet, unless
you play it to show. Even Tiresias and Cassandra's inside
dope didn't alleviate any anguish or doom. No insurance
possible for an ancient Greek. Yet I need to believe that luck
can confound fate, change its course. I need to believe you
can make a little of it out of research and nerve. The rest is
a one-time gift, a nag that for a while gave some of us hope,
like Marxism in the third.

. . .

Defeats

. . .

Those failures of nerve, not of skill, are the worst. The tentative shot. The safe position we took in the argument. Double defeats, really; where we end up on the sorry side of the score *and* our character's in question. Better to be overwhelmed and have no excuses. Even when a series of defeats sends us to the bottom of ourselves, at least there's a chance we'll locate some bedrock of dignity, a place below which we won't go. Then we can begin the long climb. Maybe we'll have learned something that can be converted into victory. Or a reason to endure. There *are* good defeats. Yet some old unexamined undercurrent, some tendency, often will return us to the scenes of our defeats. We'll dial that unhappy number we've dialed before. We'll bring up that subject that always results in shouts and tears. With luck, we'll catch ourselves, find a game we can sometimes win with someone who won't easily lose.

Acceptance

Certainly not of things as they are. Certainly not of a cosmology that posits we're insignificant, though of course we are. And aren't some of us less insignificant than others? The personal is what matters—this defeat, those mundanities, a few triumphs. And then the expansion of what personal means: another person's tragedy, a country's collapse. The larger the personal becomes the greater our helplessness. Better to be furious at one thing, become radiant with purpose. Better to love links and rhythms than all-embracing answers. I accept the croissants at breakfast and the side dish of plums. I accept that we are designed to die, and that hell is a more persuasive afterlife than heaven, though I accept neither. My friends flirt with the spiritual seductions of the East. But why would someone want to get in harmony with this universe? So much bad company. There are no escapes. Fall down seven times, stand up eight.

. . .

Notes

. . .

"I mark, stain, trespass" in "Experts" is from Allyson Clay's essay "Reflections on the Fraughtness of Painting." Used with her permission.

Some of the insect information in "Experts" and in "Advantages" is borrowed from naturalist J. B. S. Haldane.

The quotes from the Khmer Rouge torturer in "Evil" are from the archives of Pol Pot's secret prison, known as S-21, microfilmed by Cornell University, and are taken from a book in progress by Pol Pot biographer David Chandler. Used with his permission.

The quotes in "Syntax" are from Alfred Sheinwold's column in The Atlantic City *Press*, "Sheinwold on Bridge."

Though I've since been informed that the auk is extinct, I composed "Emblems" believing that it wasn't. I've left it as is. Extant or extinct, I still like the auk as an emblem.